FOREWORD BY

Love Code

Complete Checklist For Covenant Relationships

'Seun Salami

AUTHOR OF TEN TIMES BETTER & GOOD BETTER BEST

arkmedia®
and publications

LOVE CODE
Complete Checklist for Covenant Relationships

ISBN – 978-1-7752318-1-3

Published by:
Ark Media & Publications
V3S 9J7, Surrey,
BC, Canada

+1-778-885-7514
info@arkmediapublications.ca

Except otherwise stated, all scriptures are from the King James version of the bible.

Content

Foreword - v
Introduction - 9

Connection - 13
Chemistry - 19
Communication - 25
Common Interests - 35
Compatibility - 39
Contrast - 45
Conviction - 51
Confirmation - 61
Courtship - 65
Caution - 71
Centre - 77
Counsel - 85
Confession - 91
Consent - 97
Commitment - 101
Covenant - 107
Copulation - 111

This Thing Called Love - 117

Content

Foreword

Since I met my husband and we began a relationship in our early twenties, I have watched him live out and exemplify the principles he has put together in this book. One of the first things I noticed about him, apart from the fact that he looked too young and too hungry back then and not half as handsome as he is now, was that he was, and still is, very principled. I noted right away that we shared similar views when it came to opposite sex relationships and how they should be done. We agreed without any fuss that we were going into our relationship for the long term given the nature of our coming together. (We will probably share that story in detail in another book even though 'Seun shares a bit about it in the Conviction chapter). We didn't just want it to be a trial relationship, but we were committed to making it last and doing whatever it was going to take to achieve this. Although we didn't know then that life had other plans in place ahead of us to separate us for almost seven years as I had to travel to Canada to complete my education. But I'm convinced that God knew, and He brought us together just in time. We held on to God's promise during those difficult years, even when it looked practically over and eventually, God kept His word and we came back together and eventually got married. But we had a part to play and He helped us to play our part. Even when you have found the will of God for your life concerning marriage, it must still be an agreement between two people and God. So three, essentially. If either of us had given up at one point and gone on with any of the numerous suitors we were interacting with and the options that showed up during the long-distance phase of our relationship, God would have done nothing about it and it still wouldn't have made Him a liar. We had to be committed to it.

Love is commitment. It is not just about feelings. When you have feelings you have to be committed. When it seems like you don't have feelings for the person anymore, you still have to be committed. If you can do this, then you've got something. Feelings come and go. They are mostly a result of the actions of the other person, the looks, and other factors, but if you can begin your relationship on the foundation of God's word and His direction, the feelings eventually come – because feelings grow – but your foundation will be on something stronger than feelings. That is what this book is all about.

I like how simple it is, and the fact that it is very easy to read. You could read in one sitting. But I encourage you not to take the wisdom in it for granted because of that. Read it over and over until the principles become a part of you. It is small enough for you to take around with you in your bag, so do just that. Although it is a checklist of some sort, that doesn't mean you have to tick every single box, but some things are extremely important and should not be compromised.

I have heard my husband speak on several occasions right from his days as a pastor on campus till now, and I have seen him record YouTube videos where he teaches about relationships and related issues, but this is the first book he has written on love and relationships for young people, and that excites me. This is something I am also very passionate about because, so many young people are going about relationships their own way and then wonder why they make serious mistakes. Although we have many more books to come on marriage as we grow and learn ourselves as a couple, but I am glad that we can share truths from our experience of the courtship stage and how we overcome it without compromise, so others can read and know that it is possible to do courtship right, please God and be happy and fulfilled in your marriage afterwards.

Thank you for picking this book, and I know you will be greatly blessed by it. We hope to hear from you about how it has helped you. God bless you.

Dorcas 'Seun-Salami

Even when you have found the will of God
for your life concerning marriage,
it must still be an agreement
between two people and God.

Introduction

Isn't it interesting that almost all the words that accurately define true love begin with the letter C and not the letter L? From Commitment, which is probably the most important of them, to Copulation, which is possibly the most popular of them and the one most people are interested in; I have spent a good number of years, putting together these ideas until it suddenly hit me one day that every single component that constitutes true Love begins with the letter C.

But even more than the letters, what I have tried to do in this book, is to give you a simple checklist. Unassuming, yet very crucial. I have also tried to make each one as short and as straight to the point as possible without any bogus information overload or statistics that will bore you because I conceived this to be the shortest book you will ever read about love and relationships, so that you can get on with the actual relationship and doing it right. As you go through each one, try to give yourself and your relationship a mental score for that word. Again, I could have included a score sheet at the end of each chapter to say give your relationship a score from 1 to 100, but I did not. You can keep that in your head. Just make sure you have a clear idea of where you guys are with each one. The general idea is that 30% is a fail and 50% is not good enough. Just like in school. You must be able to do better than that. It doesn't also mean you have to be up there with every single point. No. There is no perfect relationship. Every single human relationship is a work in progress. You may find that you are up there in one area and doing very badly in another area. The point is that you should be able to identify this and put in work where necessary, and if it is a clear red flag, you may want to step back for a moment and reconsider. Some areas are more high risk than others. Some things are certainly worth the compromise while some others are non-negotiable. I will point these out as we go along. You also know the things that are most important to you based on your personal values. You should be looking out for these and be as honest as possible with yourself.

One of the major things I have noticed with my generation of young unmarried people is the desperation for marriage. This is very disturbing. In most cases, it is very subtle while in some other cases, it is blatant. Without prejudice to people of colour (I am one), I believe it is more prevalent amongst us. This is probably a cultural thing and largely due to our upbringing. More so, amongst ladies. It is as though we have been raised to believe that marriage is the ultimate achievement for a lady while that of a man is to be successful and be able to marry a beautiful wife. There are also those who are simply in love with the idea of being in love. It is easy to confuse this with being in love with someone. Most people just want a romantic relationship they can flaunt and be seen to be like everyone else. Permit me to make a case for a deeper perception of marriage.

You see, God never intended for marriage to be viewed as an achievement or a social trophy. There is no scripture to support that. Instead, marriage is a purposeful institution. And we see this pattern throughout scripture. Marriage is an institution set up by God to fulfil a specific purpose. Although this purpose is rather unique from couple to couple, the general reasons would be that it is an institution that mirrors the relationship between Jesus Christ and the church (Ephesians 5:25). It is also an institution that is supposed to make life easier for you to confront. Two are better than one, the bible says, because they have a good reward for their labour (Ecclesiastes 4:9). One person will chase a thousand, but when they become two, they will put ten thousand to flight. Jesus himself promised that if two people will agree as touching anything on earth, it will be done for them by God (Matthew 18:19). No wonder God looked at Adam after the creation and said in clear terms, that it is not good for him to be alone and that He would make a help meet for him (Genesis 2:18). Marriage is not an institution to be taken lightly or rushed into. I am sure you know of one or two people who did not get married in the Bible and chose instead to spend their time and energy pursuing God's agenda (1 Corinthians 7:7). I am all for marriage because it is honourable, as Hebrews 13:4 says, and it is God's holy institution which He loves (Malachi 2:11) which is why I would rather it be done the right way. With the seriousness and sobriety, it deserves, with an understanding that it is a once in a lifetime decision that is irreversible under normal circumstances and for the right reasons. The last one of these reasons I would like to mention here is procreation. Marriage is the ideal institution set up by God to fulfil the instruction He gave us which is to be fruitful and multiply. In God's original agenda, this instruction was to be carried out within the confines of marriage between a man and a woman. Anything else is an aberration and is therefore outside the will of God. There is a lot of new age ideas and concepts flying around these days and many are embracing it because it soothes the flesh, but none of these will ever change God's mind about these things. When we approach it this way, we are less likely to make mistakes that will lead to regrets in future.

Marriage was made to be enjoyed. Not endured. And I am glad you have taken one more step in preparing for that blissful future by seeking the knowledge that will make it possible. This book is not the ultimate marriage book. It was not written to be 'deep' or to impress anyone. It was written to help you. I have put down my thoughts on each subject as they have come to me, based on my experiences and years of gathering and implementing this information in my own relationship and I am confident you will find the information more than helpful in this form. I congratulate you and I look forward to hearing how the simple words in this book contributed to the big picture when your 50th marriage anniversary rolls by.

Cheers.

'Seun Salami

Connection

Human beings are created for connection, not isolation.

Boy meets Girl. I remember a famous pick-up line that almost every boy used on a girl he was interested in at one time or the other when we were growing up. "You look familiar, have we met somewhere?" The big idea was to find something that could start the conversation. Something that could break the ice. A connection. It is the same reason boys loved events like the annual inter-house sports competition back in High School. This is because students from other schools would be in attendance either to attend invitational relay races or just to watch, have fun and of course, meet the opposite sex. It provided a level playing field and it was easy to make connections with the opposite sex even if you were the shy type who would ordinarily not be able to talk to a girl without that kind of opportunity. Even the serious-minded ones who were taking part in one sporting event or the other wanted to do really well so they wouldn't need to introduce themselves when they walked up to the girl they fancied afterwards. It was all about making the right connection and making it easily. There had to be something that brought you close enough to the girl you wanted to talk to and made things easy. Maybe you attended the same tutorial, or you belonged to the same social club. In some cases, you may even have to rely on someone introducing you to the person and then things kick off from there. All I have been trying to say is that relationships begin with connection.

Human beings are created for connection, and not isolation. This is the reason why families exist. Every human being needs some form of connection and acceptance to stay alive. You need at least one person you can feel connected to. Romantic love often begins with a simple connection too. It may not be a romantic connection at first, but a common purpose or interest simply leads to a friendship that then blossoms into something serious. It could also be an emotional connection. This is what people mean when they say they like someone.

For true love to exist, there needs to be a connection between the people involved. Whether it happens on day one or day fifty-one, it needs to happen at some point. The two of you must be able to feel connected in a good way. You must feel comfortable around each other and get along quite well and more that you do with the ordinary Joe next door. You should be able to think of the person and feel comfortable (if not ecstatic) at the idea of seeing him or her again. This is where it all begins. Adolescents know a lot about this. Most of the time, when you get into a new youth group, you are immediately seeking out the people you feel most comfortable with. You are looking for the girl or guy you feel a connection with and you can chat with, at the very least, and then later it may develop into something else, but this is usually the starting point. But if you are lucky enough, you might get something quite more than connection right off the back; it is called Chemistry.

Marriage was made to be enjoyed,
not endured.

Chemistry

It is very important to have Chemistry
at some point in your relationship
even though you will require self control
to nip it in the bud until marriage.

This is the 'feelings' part of Love. It is what most people refer to when they say they have feelings for someone. Connection and Chemistry are the two major components of the Love Code that have to do with feelings. And because they are often the first ones to show up in most relationships, people get stuck on them, camp around them and build their relationships on them without going further. As good as it is to make an instant or gradual connection with someone and like them or to feel a deep sense of attraction to someone, you don't want to build a relationship that you hope will last a lifetime on that alone. Just the same way you do not build your house on green grass just because the land is so green, even though it was the greenery that attracted you to the piece of land. You must dig, and lay a solid foundation before you begin to build, if you want that house to stand the test of time. That, my dear friend, takes some time and some effort.

We can also refer to Chemistry as a spark. As the name implies, it results from the chemical components of our bodies – our hormones – because as they say, opposites attract. This is an attraction, deeper and stronger than just a connection. You see the person as someone you can be with, someone you won't mind getting close to, physically. That is Chemistry, and it is very important to have this at some point in your relationship even though you will require self control to nip it in the bud until marriage. I believe that you should not get married to someone if you don't get to this point. If you have never felt like kissing or touching the person and you only restrained yourself, then you don't have enough Chemistry to last a life time. You don't want to have to go through a mental exercise everything you need to get intimate with your husband or wife. Believe me, this happens. It should come naturally. However, it must not be the first or predominant reason for wanting to be with someone. If physical attraction is all there is to it, then that is something else and its called lust. It may be that you are only after the person for their looks or a bodily feature you desire. This isn't love at all. With love, chemistry is a part of the package, it is not the package. One major way you know if it is a part of the package is the fact that you will be able to exercise restrain despite the way you feel because there are so many other things involved. But if you find that it is an uncontrollable desire to get under the person's clothes, then you are dealing with lust. What happens in such cases is that the desire begins to fade once this urge is satisfied.

When you get into marriage, a lot of things will begin to compete with this spark, and you may find that from time to time the intensity is not the same. You will then need to become deliberate about keeping the spark going and your interest in each other alive. That is why it is dangerous to marry someone whom you do not even feel any spark for and nothing drawing you towards the person. In that case, you will have nothing to even begin to work with when things get tough later.

There is no perfect relationship.
Every single human relationship
is a work in progress.

Communication

Communication is the blood
of any relationship.

This is my favourite one of the Cs. Although I think that commitment is the most important one that truly defines the idea of love, communication is the one thing that holds everything together. Do not marry someone you do not feel comfortable communicating with. I beg you, do not. That is just like saying do not try to be a human being without blood flowing in your veins. Needless to say, this is practically impossible, right? There is no relationship without communication. Communication is the blood of any relationship. When you agree to marry someone, what you are basically saying is that I choose to communicate with this person primarily about any and everything in my life. If you deviate from that, the marriage is going to have a problem. No marriage can succeed without effective communication. Without effective communication, a relationship will die a natural death, it is only a matter of time.

Communication is usually quite easy in the beginning, especially if connection and chemistry are already in place. You want to share every and anything with the person. You find yourself having long conversations with the person, sharing pretty much everything in your heart. You spend long hours on the phone, even late into the night and the early hours of the morning. But as time goes on, and familiarity sets in, you may find that things become monotonous and you will then need to become deliberate with communication. People who have successful marriages that you envy and pray for, all have stories to tell. They worked hard at it even from their courtship, and it did not just fall on them. My wife and I know a thing or two about this. We had to do everything it took to keep communication alive during the years we lived on separate continents. Even in marriage, you will still need this. It even becomes deeper. You must be able to open up. Open up about your aspirations, your fears and your deepest challenges. The fact that communication has stopped flowing naturally does not mean you are now 'out of love', it only means you have exhausted the most obvious things you both can share about each other and it may be time to dig deeper. This is the point where many people begin to pull back and relationships begin to fall apart, because they expect that the same intensity and desire with which they were communicating from the start will continue forever if they are truly in love. Nothing is farther from the truth. Every relationship goes through the honeymoon phase when things are almost effortless before the law of diminishing returns begins to set in. This simply means that the more of something you have, the less the intensity of the desire for it. If you are hungry and you are presented with a plate of rice, you will eat it with a lot of vigour and desire. But if after the first plate is empty, a second one arrives, you will not eat with the same intensity and desire even though you may still be hungry. It doesn't mean you do not love rice. It means you

may now have to space things out and garnish more.
The importance of communication in a relationship cannot be overemphasised. It is the relationship. Without communication there is no relationship, especially if you find yourself in a distance relationship. Communication is something you will have to take seriously and be deliberate about if you want your relationship to survive, let alone thrive. When people lose hold of communication in a relationship, the relationship begins to slip from them. Both of you must be committed to communication and be comfortable communicating with each other. When you do get married, this is what will hold everything else together because you will require truthful and honest communication in different forms for everything else in your marriage to work and be effective. Without learning to communicate with each other effectively you will not even be able to pray together effectively or enjoy a good conjugal relationship, or discuss and plan the future of your children and family effectively or budget and manage the family expenses properly. Everything depends on it! This should therefore be your primary focus during your courtship. This is one of the ways you build a solid foundation for your marriage. Focus on communication. Talking to each other, asking questions, understanding each other's body language and other unspoken modes of communication. Knowing as much as possible, if not all of each other's likes and dislikes.

That said, as good as communication is, there should still be boundaries. There will be time for petting and necking in the future. You will have more than enough time to be physically intimate. Don't put the cart before the horse.

Courtship is a time of intellectual intercourse, not physical intercourse. It is the time to understand each other's body language, not each other's bodies. It is the time you should get to the bottom of your partner's mind, and not under their clothes. Don't start getting in the shower together before you are married. Don't yield to the temptation of phone sex and all these things people do these days. Don't move in with someone you are not married to. These things are wrong, regardless of how popular they have become.

If you put all of these ahead of effective communication in your relationship, you will never be able to go beyond a certain point in your communication because your physical attraction and intimacy will always get in the way. Instead of taking good advantage of the times you are alone together to talk and discuss things that will form a good foundation for your future together, it will become all about physical intimacy and undressing each other. You must be deliberate about this, if you are serious about building a happy home. The actions we take during our single years don't just go away once we get married, they are building blocks for the future, and they will show up. Sometimes we act as though everything we have done during our single days will simply vanish if we put in a good dance at the wedding reception or if we are able to organise a flawless wedding. Those things are just waiting for you in your future. That is why many people experience funny challenges in marriage they don't understand, and they begin to wonder where those things are coming from. They are simply things from your past that have come to wait for you in the future. Everything we do is an action that will produce a consequence in the future, and we must always keep this in mind. Whatever foundation you have been laying is what your home will be built on. Whatever you now begin to do after you are married only builds on this foundation and solidifies it. Make the right sacrifices now so you can enjoy the rewards later.

Let me also say that marriage usually brings out the best or worst in people, and it is whatever you have stored up inside you before you get into marriage that you will begin to display in marriage. Out of the abundance of the heart the mouth speaks (Luke 6:45). If you have been feeding your mind with negative things before marriage, it will come out in abundant measure in marriage because marriage is a 'pressure cooker'. Its just like when you put a towel in water; it absorbs water, but you don't know how much water is in that towel until you squeeze it. Marriage squeezes people. That is the reason people do certain things in marriage and surprise themselves, and then begin to blame the person they got married to as the problem.

If you give priority to communication now, you will find out that it will be easier after you are married to be naked about any issue and not be ashamed (Genesis 2:25). It will be so much easier to get to the point where you are both comfortable enough to discuss any and everything without fear or shame.

Let me also say a little about texting and chatting and our modern means of communication. It is important that you learn to have face to face conversations with the person you intend to get married to. As good and convenient as chatting and texting are, they should never replace face to face communication. Look into each other's eyes when you talk so you can see the unspoken words. You must be comfortable doing this. Again, it is something you must do deliberately. Limit chatting and texting to when you are away from each other and you can not make a phone call. Even when you are away from each other, your first choice should be a phone call and not a text or chat. Communication is more than the words. There is tone of voice, body language and other things involved in communication that you will not get from chatting. Have you also noticed how easy it is to misunderstand people when chatting and texting? You want to stay away from this as much as possible and focus on effective communication. Engage in productive conversations with your intended spouse. Build your relational skills deliberately. You will need this in marriage because there will be issues in marriage you will have to confront your spouse about and you don't want to be doing that by email or WhatsApp. There are couples who live in the same house and they communicate mostly with their phones. They cannot have decent conversations without fighting and quarrelling or allowing it to descend into something frivolous or get physical, either sexually or violently.

I have dwelt this long on communication because it is extremely important. Relational skills are one of the most important skills you need for a successful marriage, so work on that. I believe that the ability to relate effectively with your spouse is the most important skill you need for your marriage to work. The truth is that, like I mentioned earlier, you can not even pray with your spouse if you don't communicate effectively. You cannot also pray for your spouse effectively if you don't know what to pray about. And this comes from communication. Most of the issues you will face in marriage can be resolved by effective communication. You cannot sit and study the bible together because all these spiritual things require communication just as much as the physical things like sex and playing together. You are not going to be in a silent marriage. Even if you are an introvert, your spouse is the one person you must be able to talk to freely. Without this, there will be frequent conflict and things will begin to go wrong. Strive for mastery in communication with your spouse even before you get into marriage, such that you begin to understand each other beyond words. That is the point where you know the unspoken words of the other person. You know when they are angry, hungry, upset or in need of something even when they aren't talking. You will avoid unnecessary quarrels and only have to deal with the important things in marriage.

One good place to begin communication from is the place of your common interests.

Do not marry someone you do not feel comfortable communicating with.

Common Interests

Your passions and goals must align, even if the methods of achieving them are different.

One of the greatest marriage advice you will ever receive is that you should marry your best friend. I am sure you have heard that before. What that means is that you should find someone who loves things you love and hates the things you hate. You may have differences, but anything you have such strong emotional connection to as to be able to say you love this or hate these other things, make sure your partner feels the same way about these things, otherwise you are setting yourself up for endless conflicts. If you love kids for instance to the extent that you can consider adopting one, you have no business with someone who cannot stand kids. This is extremely important. You can disagree on the colour to pick for his wedding suit or what colour your house will be, but not on an issue as important as whether to have kids or if adoption is something you are open to. Your passions and goals must align in some way, even if the methods you are employing in achieving them are different. You must be heading in the same direction. If for instance, you are hanging around a guy who loves to support a certain cause, and you know this cause is the farthest thing from your heart, you need to have a rethink rather than banking on the fact that you might be able to convince him to look in a different direction. Our true passions never really go away until we have been able to do something significant about them. You will remain unhappy and hollow for a long time until the day you are able to truly begin to live out your life's purpose. So, once you notice that your intended spouse is heading in a passionate direction, you must ask yourself if this is a direction that appeals to you.

There must be (good) things you both do together and you both enjoy doing, especially together. Again, there may be a few things you do simply because your partner likes to do these things and you are only doing them to please him or her, but there must be things you both enjoy, things you have in common and feel the same way about. My wife became interested in soccer because of how passionate I am about soccer and the club I support and I had to do the same for a few things I didn't really like initially, but we both love and feel the same level of passion for God and His word. This is our major common ground. We both thrive on this and enjoy doing the things of God. As much as possible, make sure your common interests are in the areas that carry the most significance. You can disagree on minor areas, but do not compromise on the most important things.

Compatibility

Every relationship needs a fair share of differences to survive.

Compatibility means that the both of you can live together in harmony. I like to talk about compatibility as your differences divided by your common interests. Every relationship needs a fair share of differences to survive. But the ratio of differences in comparison to your common interests, in a way, is what is referred to as compatibility. Differences must not extremely outweigh common interests. There must be a balance for any relationship to work. Another way to look at it would be to ask the question, how well do you complement each other and make up for each other's weaknesses. You may not like to do everything the same way, but where one falls short, the other must be able to fill in, in a way that makes the both of you seem like one unit. That is what compatibility is about and not that you must both like the same things and love to do the same things all the time. That is called common interests and it is just as important, but being compatible with someone is much more than that. It is the blending of just enough of both differences and likes, just enough to makes you both able to live together in harmony and complement each other, even though you are two complete people coming together in marriage.

Compatibility doesn't also mean there would be no quarrels. If anything, it guarantees it. But there should be no differences that are deemed irreconcilable. If that exists before you get married, it should be a red flag. Don't do it. It means you are not compatible with the person. The gravity of the differences clearly outweigh the common interests. There will be many things you would absolutely love about the person and some other things you may need to tolerate for the sake of the things you like about the person. But there must never be something you know you simply cannot live with and still go ahead to marry the person just because you must get married. That is a no. There must be a healthy dose of friendship and friendliness and just the right amount of differences for both of you to get along just fine and be able to live together. You cannot both agree on everything and always see things the exact same way, otherwise your relationship will lack perspective and it will be difficult to make real progress. For instance, you may not have the exact same spending habits. This is healthy for a relationship because while one person might be a spend thrift, the other is a prudent one who puts the balance in when necessary. That said, if giving is a value you hold dear for instance, make sure that as much as there is going to be a balance, you are getting married to someone who is not so stingy that you will be unable to give out anything you both own. This can lead to serious dissatisfaction in marriage.

This becomes even more important in interracial marriages. There is nothing wrong with getting married to someone from a different race if there is the right mix of common interests and differences. The chances of differences only increase in such cases because of your different backgrounds so you want to pay close attention to the things that matter to you the most and be sure you can handle any cultural differences that exist.

How well do you complement each other and make up for each other's weaknesses?

Contrast

You are two unique individuals coming together in a marriage union to complement each other.

Balance is one of the most important things in life and in relationship. As we explained with compatibility, your traits must provide good contrast in certain areas. If you end up with someone who only wants the things you like and does not have a mind of their own or just enough differences in certain areas, there will be no balance in your relationship. One person might have an extremely analytical mind while the other is emotional. One person might love to work with numbers while the other prefers words. It doesn't mean that if the two of you are both literary people then your relationship will not work, but it means that there must be other areas where you have differences that are not serious enough to be deal breakers, but can add value to your relationship and make it a rounded one. That is the point. That you are two unique individuals coming together in a marriage union to complement each other.

I am reminded of a movie most of us watched while growing up, in which an African prince was presented with a potential bride from one of the maidens in the kingdom in a colourful ceremony and then he asked to have a moment with his bride-to-be. When they got into the room, he began to ask her questions about her likes and dislikes and all she could say to everything he said was "whatever you like" as though she had no mind of her own, all the while hopping and barking at his orders. Needless to say, he decided against marrying her and chose instead to take a trip to another part of the world to find a woman who will be her own person and love him for the person he was and not the fact that he was a rich prince.

This is also a good place to speak again about interracial relationships. There are several challenges that people feel such relationships pose, but I strongly believe that contrast is one of the blessings of mixed race marriages and this is beneficial for the children and the family. They will be able to look at and address issues differently based on their backgrounds and not just a narrow view of things. If such couples view it as a strength rather than a weakness, they can experience and benefit from the richness in their diversity.

Let me also say a little about conflict and conflict resolution here, just because I don't want to make it a separate chapter. There is no relationship immune to conflict. If there is no conflict at all in your relationship, wait for it, because it will surely show up at some point. Conflicts are a legitimate part of relationships. It is your response to these conflicts that is extremely important. The period of courtship is the time to develop conflict resolution. You must get to know this person enough to know how best to resolve the conflicts with him or her. Practise this and be quick to resolve issues before they blow up. Don't get into the habit of waiting for the other person to be the one to apologise every time there is a misunderstanding regardless of who is to blame. If this is becoming an issue in your relationship, talk about it. This is one of the areas of maturity needed for a successful marriage.

There is no relationship immune to conflict.
If there is no conflict at all
in your relationship, wait for it.

Conviction

Conviction is being fully persuaded about a course of action usually because of a superior argument or an evidence.

Let us move on now to a very serious aspect of the subject of choosing a life partner. Conviction is one major thing that people no longer seek for their relationships. They are okay with feelings and they ride with this. No wonder marriages no longer last. Conviction is a firm belief in the rightness (or wrongness, if I can use that word) of something. Being fully persuaded about a course of action usually because of a superior argument or an evidence. This is so important.

There is no better place therefore to receive a conviction about anything than the one who created you and created the one you are seeking to go into marriage with. He is the only one that can provide you with that superior argument or evidence you need to hold on to. The assurance that you are doing the right thing, with the right person, and at the right time. This is more than just having peace about something. I say that because it is possible to be stealing and have peace about it if your conscience is seared. Also, when you are not working after the spirit but after your flesh, it is difficult to know if the "peace" you feel is from the satisfaction of having something you have always desired or from heaven.

So, what am I saying? Whether you are the type that believes that God can speak to people about who to marry or you are not, you need a conviction from God. Regardless of how you made your choice, you still have to take it to God in prayer and let him give you an assurance (usually from His word) that when you pass through the fire and water in that union, He will be with you and it will not burn you, or that you should be still and know that He is God. There is a lot of mockery these days about the idea of people receiving their life partners directly from God, because some have abused the idea and many others have tried to use this falsely to satisfy the desires of their flesh. However, this does not change the fact that God still speaks to people about who to marry. If He speaks about other things and you believe it is from God, why is it so difficult to believe He can speak about this? There are a few problems I see. First, most people are not in the place where God can speak to them. They neglect their relationship with God and hearing His voice until it is time to choose a life partner and then they say they cannot hear God. The other problem is simply laziness. People in our generation are too lazy to seek God for themselves. They would rather that the Pastor goes to seek God for them and then come tell them "thus says the Lord". The major reason why many cannot benefit from this grace that is available, is the fact that many people wait until it is time to make big decisions before trying to hear from God. It must have been a lifestyle, where you have trained yourself in the art of hearing from God in the way that He speaks to you, and you must have confirmed this severally with little things, before you get to this point. If you have not learnt how to be led by the Holy Spirit, it is usually too late to start when it is time to choose a life partner. But if you are one of the few exceptions, and you have been able to maintain a relationship with God and like Jesus said, you are a sheep that knows the voice of the good shepherd, I celebrate with you, because there is no better way to decide on a choice than the one the Lord himself reveals. So, go to Him and ask and He will answer. This is how I knew that Dorcas was going to be my wife. The Spirit of God spoke this to my spirit one night as I prayed.

Let me give you a little background to my walk with God just because I need you to really understand this. I got born-again very early in my life. I was born a Muslim, but my mother became a Christian somewhere along the line and I became exposed to the Bible and the things of God. I was thirteen when I first really understood and accepted the gospel of Jesus, but I became very serious about my faith in God at some point during High School in Kings College, Lagos. I started attending healing crusades and meetings like that from school and then after I left the boarding house, I started attending church regularly at home. By the time I got water baptised a few years later, I already knew I had a call of God on my life. Before then, I had already begun to lead a teenagers' church and I had preached my first message in the adults' church of the parish I was attending when I was still only fifteen years old. I was already learning how to hear from God at that point. I was baptised in the Holy Spirit from High School. I already had a culture of personal prayer and bible study time. Sometimes I would be lost in my bible for eight straight hours at once. I knew how to hear from God already and by the time I got into

Lagos State University for my first degree, I was hearing from God about a lot of things and I wrote down those things every day as I prayed so I could be sure when they happened. I still have the journals where I wrote those things till this day. I was already operating in the word of knowledge while pastoring the teenagers church with many testimonies to confirm this precious gift of the spirit. In fact, the department I ended up in at Lagos State University was a testimony in itself. God had told me that he was sending me to the Mass Communication department on an assignment for Him. After I wrote the matriculation examination, I was admitted to study English Language, despite the fact that my first choice was Mass Communication. But I knew what God had told me, and I held on to this even though doubts were beginning to set in, and as a human being, I was somewhat glad that I may just have escaped this mysterious assignment God had for me in the School of Communication. I went ahead and began my registration process in the English Department and we already even paid my acceptance fees. Until one day, my mother got a phone call that another list was out, and I had been admitted to the Mass Communication department.

At the end of my first year leading to the start of my second year, I became the President of the school fellowship in a mysterious way. The leader of the fellowship handed over the fellowship to my care, supposedly temporarily, on the grounds that he was going to be away for some time. I never saw him again. The next time I saw his face, it was on an obituary poster in front of the school gate announcing that he had gone home to be with the Lord. I remember weeping like a child and rolling on the floor right there in front of the school with people trying hard to comfort me. They couldn't have understood what was going on. I was grieved in more ways than one. I was heartbroken that I had lost someone who was already becoming a mentor to me in the one year I had spent in school, and then I was also afraid, because the work was now going to be my responsibility. I had never done anything in that capacity before, apart from my little teenagers' church before I got into the university. It was a really strange situation. But then I remembered what God had told me about the assignment He had for me there, and I went back to Him for the wisdom and courage to do the work, and I believe I did it faithfully and effectively for two years before moving on to an advisory capacity in my final year. All through all of these, I had built a practical lifestyle of hearing and obeying God in my personal life and with leading the fellowship.

I have told you this story to let you see that this was already a lifestyle for me and so when God spoke to me about Dorcas at a time when I was not even praying for a wife (because I already had someone I felt I loved, that my family even knew and we were going to end up together when we grew older – that too is a different story for another day), I knew it had to be God. And then Dorcas also heard from God and received her own confirmation. She had also learnt how to do that before we met. She already served as the Vice President of her own school fellowship during her pre-degree as well and was even more fervent for God than I was, even with all I just shared with you about myself. So, if you are not yet at a point where you are looking to get married, my best advise for you would be to get serious with God and learn how to hear from Him. Not just so that when the time comes to get married you will get direction from God, but it is something you will need for the rest of your life. So that is the first, and best way, to get a conviction.

That said, there is also nothing wrong with seeing a lady or guy you like and desiring to marry him or her. That is why we are given free will to make choices and be ready to face the consequences of our choices. But to get a conviction concerning your choice, you need to still take it to God and ask that His will be done and spend time praying about it. Let me also say that it is never too early to begin praying for your life partner. Even if you have not met the person, you can begin to pray for him or her. In fact, this is the best time to do this. This is a wise approach. Pray for your lines to fall in pleasant places, and that only the will of God will be done concerning your marriage and union. You can also pray for the signs that will show you the person that God has prepared for you, so that you will not be confused when the time comes because God is not the author of confusion. When the time comes, and people begin to put pressure on you from all quarters, you will know what God has shown you and you can weigh your options against this, so you don't make a mistake. At a certain age, pressure to get married comes from every direction; from your parents, your friends getting married, your biological clock ticking and all the rest. You want to be prepared before this time. You want to have sown seeds of prayer into your future that will speak for you at the right time. If you don't make deposits, there would be nothing to draw from when the time comes. One thing I have noticed about this issue of pressure is that sometimes it comes out of love and concern for you, but unfortunately, most people get married to whoever they are dating at the point where the pressure to get married is highest. Many others end up with a desperate choice either because they didn't find the so called right person or they were not just 'lucky' with relationships. Prayer can take care of that, especially prayers that are offered long before it becomes an urgent matter. It is foolishness to begin to lay a foundation when the flood is near. And if you have met the person and you are preparing for marriage, you can start praying specific prayers for your home, your children, your finances, the challenges that will come and every single aspect of your relationship. Prayer is an advantage for a child of God and it is one most people do not make use of. Jesus said even the heathens pray (Matthew 6:7), so why do children of God not pray?

You should also ideally submit this choice or interest to your spiritual leader to help pray about and direct you on the best way to go about it, especially if you both belong to the same assembly of believers. The bible says we should do things decently and in order (1 Corinthians 14:40). This is what differentiates us from the people of the world. It is when people have hidden motives that they feel funny about presenting such things in the open. It will help you to be accountable and not make some unnecessary mistakes. When you have received your own conviction, you can now seek a confirmation from your spiritual leader, your parents, friends you can trust who know the Lord and have no personal interest or stake in the matter.

Many people wait until it is time to make big decisions before trying to hear from God.

Confirmation

"If you keep thinking about something, you will dream about it."

Throughout God's word – the old testament and the new – we see a lot of emphasis on the idea of two or three witnesses, and that it is at the mouth of two or three witnesses that every matter is established (Deuteronomy 19:15, Matthew 18:16, 2 Corinthians 13:1). After you get a conviction for your relationship, you need to ask God to confirm His word by the mouth of two or three witnesses, so it can be established in your heart and on the earth. You also need to give room for this confirmation. Don't go about selling your conviction so much to everyone and then expect a confirmation from these same people. Help yourself to put yourself on the right path. Neutral people are usually the best sources of confirmation. People who have no vested interest in the issue at hand.

You can have dreams and visions about your relationship, but you cannot really depend on these, especially if you are already emotionally invested in the relationship. Your dreams can come through a multitude of activities. I like the CEV translation of Ecclesiastes 5:3, it says, "If you keep thinking about something, you will dream about it." Therefore, you can't depend on a dream you had where you saw yourself drowning and it was this person who came to rescue you. Every dream must be tested and confirmed, and it must align with the word of God. God's word is the ultimate dream or vision.

Courtship

Courtship is a time of intellectual intercourse, not physical intercourse.

Courtship is the final stage of your relationship before marriage. Courtship is primarily for the purpose of getting to know someone before marriage. Getting to understand each other as much as possible and laying a good foundation for your marriage.

As we established earlier, your focus during Courtship should be on communication and getting to understand this other human being who grew up differently and has a completely different upbringing from yours. During courtship you need to see each other under different situations and circumstances that bring out the best and worst in you. You need time to understand people and intensity to observe.

People have given several timelines that are appropriate for courtship and different people have their reasons for what they recommend. Some who recommend a minimum timeframe as soon as six months say it is better to have a very short courtship to avoid the temptation of falling into sexual sin. As good as this sounds, I believe six months is too short to really know someone. Besides, the purpose of Courtship is not to avoid sexual sin but to get to know someone. Avoiding sexual sin should be settled in the hearts and minds of the people involved and they should work together to achieve this. Dorcas and I did this from the very beginning of our relationship and invited God to help us in this resolve. What is the point of having a short courtship in order not to sin and then missing out on the true essence of courtship by going into marriage in a hurry with someone you don't really know and having to confront all sorts of issues later?

On the other hand, there are those who say that long courtship is better because it gives you enough time to know someone. Although some people can pretend effectively even over a long period of time, I lean more towards this school of thought. I believe that a minimum period of one year is ideal. This is just me and it is not a doctrine. I believe the longer you spend in courtship, the greater your chances of knowing each other better before marriage. It gives you more time to see each other in different situations and circumstances and to study each other and prepare adequately. You do not have to be in a relationship for seven years before you get married - like Dorcas and I had to, ours was circumstantial - but the length of time has its advantages. You need to see the good, the bad and the ugly about this person and know that you can handle these things and not just jump to a conclusion that things will be okay, after all, you love each other. Jumping to conclusion is the laziest form of knowledge acquisition. You need unique circumstances to see unique behaviours. You need to know how this person relates with his friends, his parents, his siblings, his colleagues, his superiors, his spiritual leaders and such like. Does he or she even have a spiritual leader? Does he or she believe that you have to be accountable to someone and be under authority? By being in different situations and circumstances, you will see behavioural traits you will not ordinarily see by going on dates in nice restaurants and vacationing on a beach in the Bahamas.

Still, nothing guarantees that you will not have challenges in your marriage. The best of us are still human. Every marriage has its fair share of challenges, but a rushed courtship gives you even less time to prepare for this. Having said all that, whatever local assembly you belong to, I believe you will do well to follow the guidelines there. Many times when God puts us in a church family (Psalm 68:6) it is for two main reasons. It is because we have something the church needs, and secondly and often most importantly, it is because the church has something we need (either for our present or our future - Psalm 92:13). Finally, if you have the Holy Spirit of God in you, he will guide you into all truth.

Every marriage has its fair share of challenges,
but a rushed courtship gives you
even less time to prepare for this.

Caution

Courtship is not the same thing as marriage,
so the privileges of marriage must
still be saved for marriage.

Even after you have gotten a confirmation and you are now officially in courtship, there is still the need to exercise caution in so many areas. First, you must understand that a courtship is not the same thing as marriage, so the privileges of marriage must still be saved for marriage. This is not the time to begin to live together as has become the norm in the western world. This is not pleasing to God in anyway and for any reason. The sole purpose of courtship is to get to know each other better and build a good foundation for a healthy marriage. The purpose is not to experiment with each other's bodies or get physically intimate. There is the tendency to begin to think at this stage that since you are getting married anyway, it is okay to get physical with each other. Or since everyone knows you are getting married, it is okay to do certain things. I like to say that the fact that you are getting married anyway is the reason you should be able to wait for it. You will belong to each other for the rest of your lives anyway, so why not just endure the few months that remain and get into marriage without any form of guilt.

That you are in a courtship is not a guarantee that it would lead to marriage, no matter how advanced your relationship becomes. People change their minds days before their wedding and things happen in life. Some people don't even show up for their weddings. One major purpose of courtship is to identify possible deal breakers before you go into marriage. It is at this stage that most people remember to carry out blood tests and find out about their suitability for marriage, medically. It is another area of compatibility that is often ignored until the last minute.

Don't be in a hurry to get married. Take your time and keep your eyes open. The way I like to say it is that you should keep your eyes wide open before you get married, so that you can close your eyes to your partner's faults after you get married. This may be the only time you will be able to discover certain things at a stage you can still do something about it. Many couples have been known to stop trying to please each other after a few years of marriage and then several flaws begin to emerge that put a strain on the relationship. There is little or nothing that can be done in most cases, at that stage. Now is the time you must observe, watch and pray.

If you notice any dangerous tendencies, especially of violence and anger, don't sweep it under the carpet and make excuses because of your desperation to get married. Address and confront those issues. There is no man who has ever raised his hands to beat up his wife that did not leave little clues before they got married. In many cases, some of these signs only begin to show up after the wedding date has been picked and the stress begins to mount, revealing cracks. However, because there is already a date, all these signs will be completely ignored. The fact that you have picked a wedding date does not mean the wedding cannot be postponed or cancelled. You must weigh your options and decide if your life is more important to you than having a society wedding just to please people. If you discover something that is a red flag, it is only wise that you stop to consider it with the advise of people who should know better than you. No one will come to your rescue when these things come back to hunt you after you get married.

Keep your eyes wide open
before you get married, so that you can
close them to your partner's faults
when you get married.

Centre

God will never give you anything
that will replace Him in your life.

Every human relationship has a heart. A centre. It is what drives that relationship and the very thing that either brought the both of you together or is keeping you together. You not only need to know what the centre of your relationship is, you must be deliberate about what it is (even if the reason that brought you both together is far from genuine). Here is what I mean. You need to ask yourselves, truthfully, what is the one thing that is keeping you in that relationship? More often that not, that is what the heart of the relationship is. And it could be anything from money, to sex, to even God. There are three main things that could predominantly be the centre of your relationship from time to time and I will share that with you in this chapter. One major way to find out what this is, is to answer this question: what is it you do the most whenever you both are alone together, and you are almost certain that no one will ever find out? This is often the strongest pointer to what the centre (the heart) of your relationship is. If you take that thing away, the relationship begins to lose meaning, and it soon begins to feel like you can do without that person because you no longer have that thing that is keeping you together. This is a very important matter to deal with, especially while you are still in courtship, but it is rarely taught. You must be honest with yourselves and find out what that thing is, and if it is not something you are proud about, then you need to fix it, deliberately and replace it with something that represents a solid foundation on which to build a lasting relationship.

Once you can effectively define who or what is at the driving seat of your relationship from time to time (because it can change per time), it will help put you in check regularly and help you know where you are headed in that relationship.

You must always strive to remain in the perfect will of God in your relationship at all times. What takes the driver's seat of your relationship per time is determined by what you allow or permit, and at every given time, the three things that could be the centre of your relationship, is either:

- GOD (or Godliness),
- SEX (or Sexual Pleasure) or
- YOUR PARTNER (or things that come from your partner).

I like to differentiate between sex and sexual pleasure a lot because there are those who believe that they are doing great because they are not having actual sex even though they are doing almost everything else except the actual act of penetration. If it gives you sexual pleasure, it is in this bracket. Godliness refers to Godly activities just in the same way and your partner includes anything, like money or companionship, that comes directly from your partner.

So, your relationship is always centred around either of

these three things or these three areas and this is what determines the foundation and direction of your relationship and what goes on in it. Again, I ask you; What do you do most often when the both of you are alone together? The truthful answer you give will provide us with a clear clue and we can draw either of three conclusions:

- If it is sex or sexual pleasure, then your relationship is built on Lust.
- If it is God or Godly activities, your relationship is most likely built on Love, because God is love (1 John 4:8).
- If it is anything that is majorly about either of you or satisfying your physical needs and desires, your relationship is probably built on Infatuation.

Let me use these diagrams to drive home my point visually:

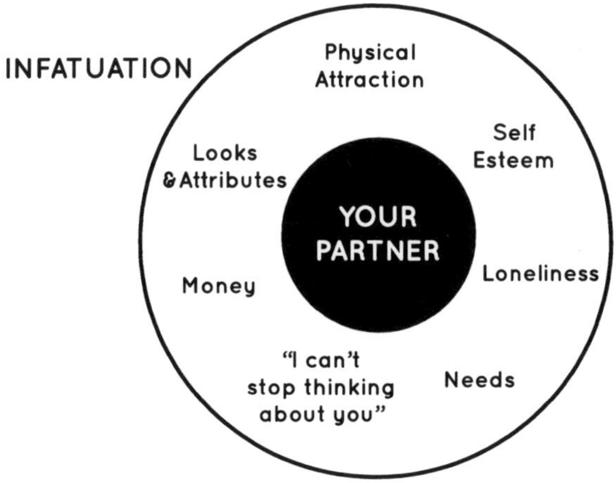

LUST

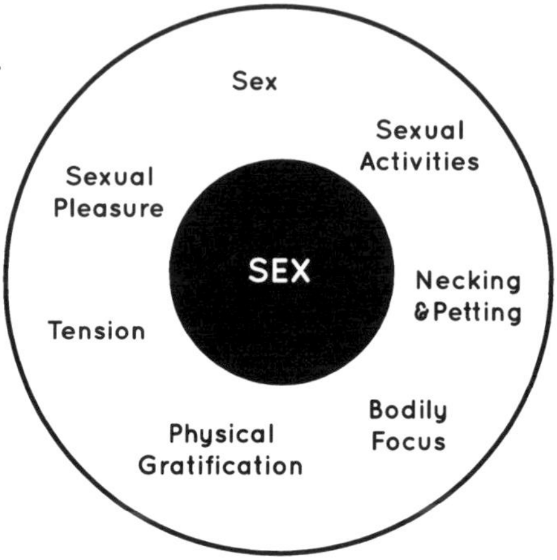
Sex
Sexual Activities
Sexual Pleasure
SEX
Necking & Petting
Tension
Bodily Focus
Physical Gratification

LOVE

Commitment
Mutual Respect
Prayer
GOD
Giving
Shared Values
Virtues & Principles
Questions & Conversations

At any and every given point in time, you can locate your relationship in any of these three zones. Where is yours at the moment? Always give God first place in your relationship. Your partner should only be second to God in your life because you are both mere mortals and you have a creator. God is a jealous God (Exo 20:5; 34:14). He has not changed. He wouldn't take kindly to making another man or woman more important in your life than He is to you. You show this by your actions and not just with words. By what you spend most of your time on. What you give most of your resources to. God will never give you anything that will replace Him in your life.

If all that is keeping you together right now are the good looks, some physical endowments or the good things of life you enjoy by being with this person, I can assure you that beauty does fade and it happens to both men and women. When people say love is blind, I let them know that marriage will open their eyes, and this doesn't take many years. The courtship stage is the best time to make God the centre of your relationship, give it a strong foundation built around the one who initiated the idea of a man and woman coming together. Don't you think He should know what works best? It is the values, virtue, trust and commitment that you build now that will sustain your relationship over time.

Sex can never and will never be a proof of genuine love. It only clouds your sense of judgement. There is a simple question I usually like to ask any guy who wants sex from a lady to prove she loves him.

"Do you love your mum?"

I'm sure you know the sharp answer anyone would give to that. "Of course."

Then I ask, why haven't you slept with her to prove that you love her. You cannot even conceive that, right? So, sex does not prove love. The real test of love is the ability to wait. The ability to wait, not just for something, but to wait because of something. These are two different things. You are waiting with the person, and not just waiting for the person while you do other things and sample other ladies or date other guys on the side. It is about remaining faithful and truthful while you wait. This is the dimension of love we don't hear about anymore. People just want to do whatever feels right to them. If you love something, you will preserve and guard it jealously. You will wait.

By the time you get married, these feelings may fade and you will begin to see clearly. Be wise my friend. Build your relationship on the right foundation. It is your responsibility.

Counsel

You may be young, but you don't have to go into marriage as a novice.

Getting married is probably the most dangerous decision you can make without wise counsel. In the multitude of counsellors, there is safety. Without good direction, people lose their way; the more wise counsel you follow, the better your chances (Proverbs 24:16). The same thing is repeated in Proverbs 11:14 - Where no counsel is, the people fall: but in the multitude of counsellors there is safety.

After you get a conviction and you have received confirmation of your choice, you need wise counsel from people who have succeeded and are succeeding in their own marriage. Ask them questions and prepare your heart for what is ahead. If you attend a bible based church, I assume your church would have a programme in place that helps intending couples prepare for marriage. Register for that, attend and pay attention studiously. So many people are usually not told much about getting married and raising children, and you may not be told too except you ask questions. Many times, older people feel they may be giving a wrong impression of marriage to younger folks if they tell you the difficulties to expect, so you may need to ask. It is not all rosy and you want to be prepared for any challenges that lie ahead. It is true that experience is the best teacher, especially when you can simply learn from the experience of others without having to go through the same thing or make the same mistakes just to learn the lesson. For instance, no one can prepare you adequately for welcoming a new born baby into your home. I can write another book on that experience. I have had it twice now, and I am grateful to God for each one. But it is not as colourful as the Instagram pictures suggest. It is an experience that changes you, but older couples are usually silent about things like that except you ask pointed questions. Thankfully I had read a little about it and I knew what to expect and do. The more prepared you are for even the little things, the better your chances of succeeding at them.

Don't go into marriage with just the ideas you got from Hollywood. Those things usually create expectations that conflict with the reality and uniqueness of your own marriage and you then begin to wonder if you are the problem or you made a wrong choice. Many of the issues young couples face can be taken care of by wise counsel so make it a deliberate part of your courtship. Find an older couple you can look up to and learn from. Ask them keen questions and get as much understanding as possible. If you ask good questions, you will get good answers.

Take advantage of any opportunity you get to attend marriage conferences and seminars organised by credible God-fearing people with proofs in their own marriages. Look for these opportunities and make yourself available to attend. You learn a whole lot from such events. Read up on marriage, just like you are doing now, and learn about the role you will be playing in your home. You may be young, but you don't have to go into marriage as a novice. You can understand a lot by books and it will seem as though you are wiser than your years. There is a lot of information in good books that will help you and save you so much time and wasted effort. Don't take anything for granted and don't leave things to chance when it comes to preparing for your marriage. This is a price that people who have successful marriages pay. You need information on how marriage works, and you must put in the work required. You need to know the challenges that other people have faced in marriage and how they have overcome these. If the next thing in your life at this stage is the issue of marriage, this should be your sole focus at this point. You shouldn't even be reading about anything else until you have considerable knowledge and information on marriage. Too many young people go into marriage blindly, with lofty expectations they get from movies and romance novels which later create conflict in their marriage when these expectations are not met.

I believe that the choice of who to marry is the single most important decision you will make in your life. I know it is true that the decision to give your life to Christ and become a child of God is what you have always known to be the most important decision in your life, but I put it to you, that the person you get married to can determine whether you have your prayers answered (1 Peter 3:7) and ultimately even derail you from making heaven. It is therefore, in that sense, more important than even your salvation decision. There are people who gave their lives to Christ and later went back into sin and into the world to do some terrible things, and after a while, maybe they heard a good message and they were convicted by the Holy Spirit to come back to God. Do you know that when such people return to God, he practically wipes away everything in their past and gives them a new beginning? (Isaiah 1:18, Hebrews 8:12; 10:17). Many of them go on to become mighty for God regardless of their past. But when it comes to marriage, people hardly get over divorce, and God hates it, according to Malachi 2:16. Some people argue that Christians make a big deal of divorce, yet it is just like any other sin. They forget that stealing someone's pen does not have the same effect on the person as divorce. That scripture in Malachi goes on to say that divorce covers one's garment with violence. The New Living Translation says when you divorce your wife, you overwhelm her with cruelty. It damages a part of people's souls and a root of bitterness is planted. This is the reason why most people who have been divorced go on to have more than one more marriage. I am just trying to let you understand the gravity of the issue and why you cannot go into it blindly and without counsel because you do not know half of what you need to know to have a successful marriage, but that information is out there, and you need to find it. Please pay serious attention to this decision, it is the most important decision you will ever make in your life.

Confession

Make up your mind that you will not keep secrets from your spouse.

How much of this person's secrets do you know and how much of yours have you been able to comfortably reveal? You may not have been able to reveal everything, but you must feel comfortable enough to reveal the things that are most important to the decision you are about to make, especially the things that happened to the both of you or that you did while you were not in each other's lives. Too many marriages start out on the foundation of falsehood, little wonder most usually hit a road block too soon. Because as humans, we try to always put our best foot forward for fear of rejection, we fail to completely open up ourselves so that the other person can see the good, the bad and the ugly side of us and then make an informed decision. You may have gotten attracted to someone because of the good things, but until you learn of the bad and ugly things, you cannot really say you are truly in love with someone. There are things you will learn of that will require some time for you to accept and come to terms with, while others may be deal breakers. Someone once said that a broken courtship is better than a broken marriage. It is better you confess those secrets now even if it has to be systematic or with the help of some form of authority over you, than wait until you are married. If such things come to the open then, it would appear you only deceived the person into marrying you. Even if they do not end the marriage, I guarantee you, you will be living with a person whose heart has shifted from you for the rest of your life. It will take heaven and earth to rebuild trust in your marriage, and without trust there can not be true oneness.

You can begin to build trust even before you get married. You do this by learning to be open and honest about everything. Make up your mind that you will not keep secrets from this person. Don't be one of those promoting the idea of individuality in marriage. There is nothing like that. Two will become one, is what the Bible says (Ephesians 5:35). If you love your individuality so much, you shouldn't bother getting married because nothing destroys a marriage faster than selfishness. You must be selfless. This is the reason many married people live secretive lives even though they are married. Their spouses cannot go near their phones, their computers have three layers of passwords, their entire lives are built on secrets; these things don't foster trust and oneness in a marriage. One of the most important areas of openness is money, because money is another major marriage destroyer. From your courtship, you should be able to tell how your partner approaches money and views money. Again, your values must align in this area.

The other aspect of confession I want to touch on is the confession of your love for each other. At the point in your relationship when you have received an assurance that this is the person you are spending the rest of your life with, love should be growing. And one of the ways love grows is when you confess your love for each other regularly. In fact, the actual definition of the word courtship is the wooing of one another – the period where this wooing takes place. This is the period where you compliment each other and say nice things to each other even as you are looking out for differences that should be straightened out, don't neglect the good things or take them for granted. This is easy at the beginning, but like most other things in marriage, you must become deliberate about it as time goes on otherwise it begins to fade in your heart. This becomes extremely important once your relationship gets to the commitment stage, because that is really and truly what love is, and saying it to each other regularly will reaffirm it in your hearts and cause it to grow. It should not just be a meaningless cliché you use to end phone calls, but something you say to each other consistently and deliberately, especially face to face.

Saying 'I love you' should not just be
a meaningless cliché you use
to end phone calls.

Consent

Marriage is not just the union of the two
of you as individuals, but a union
of the two families as well.

Too many young people in this generation are comfortable with the idea of getting married without the consent of their parents. This is wrong. God is not pleased with this. He says we should honour our parents so that our days may be long. (Exodus 20:12). Seeking and getting their consent for your choice of a life partner is one important way to do this. I understand that it may be difficult sometimes, but you must make up your mind to do what it takes to get their blessing, or at the very least, their consent. If it means waiting and praying until they have a change of heart, then so be it. The truth is that what an elder sees while seated, a child cannot see even if he climbs a tall tree. Their concerns are often genuine, but we are sometimes blinded by our desire and love for the person we want to get married to. Marriage is not just the union of the two of you as individuals, but a union of the two families as well. It is primarily about the two of you becoming one, no doubt, but you will not be able to get away from your families as long as they are alive. You will have his or her parents as your parents too and both families also become one in a way. There is no harm in taking a step back and considering their concerns objectively, it will only strengthen your love and union more if you confront challenges and you are able to overcome them, rather than avoiding them. You must seek to get the blessings of your parents for your marriage. Civilisation and modernity does not negate this in any way.

It is also important to get the consent of your spiritual parents as well. Ideally, they should have been part of the journey from the start anyway. But if not, at least let them give their consent and blessing. As wise as we think we are in this generation because of the advancement in technology and all of the new age thinking around us, there is still so much we do not know and so much we can learn if we humble ourselves to listen and seek advise from those who have been down the road we intend to travel. This is wisdom.

Also seek the consent of your trusted friends and be open to honest remarks without blacklisting any one for giving you their honest opinion. It doesn't mean you have to take every advise, but at least put things together with an open mind and weigh those things against your conviction.

Commitment

Love is not a feeling, it is a decision.
It is a decision you make
to be committed to someone.

If there is one word that accurately captures what true love entails, it is commitment. Love is commitment. Love is not a feeling, it is a decision. It might – and should - involve feelings, as we've clearly established, but it is not a feeling and should not be confused as such. It is a decision you make to be committed to someone, regardless of the circumstances that currently exist or will exist in the future, and the ability to stick to that decision. It is a sense of pledge and obligation. That is what true love is about because when everything else goes away, either momentarily or permanently, that is what will keep you going.

Another word I can use to describe this is the word devotion. It is not the type you have every morning when you read your bible and pray. That's not what I'm talking about. I am talking about a profound, unwavering and uncompromising dedication to someone. That is what love is. Being devoted to someone. Being ready to give whatever it takes to see the other person well and happy. Putting the other person first, all the time, even before yourself. That is love.

Love is giving. The word used to describe love in the bible (Agape – the God kind of love), also means to give. That is why there is no true love without giving, and the greatest gift one can give another person is one's life. Greater love hath no man than this, that a man should lay down his life for his friends (John 15:13). One must also be able to give one's word and keep it, provided it still means something.

So, your relationship moves to the commitment stage now. There is no going back. You both know and understand that. You are both committed to this, with God. You will make it work. You are no longer in doubt at this stage. This is the ideal time to start to talk about marriage and picking dates, this is where families get to know one another, and things start to move along. And this is what scares a lot of guys, especially those who are really not ready and are just messing around. This is where you know whether you are with a boy or a man. If your relationship has clearly advanced to the commitment stage and he is refusing to commit, you may just be on a ride. If he really wants it, he will not be afraid to put a ring on it. Commitment is one of the things God used to keep myself and Dorcas together throughout our difficult period. And it started in a funny little way. I remember giving her a ring back then, almost as soon as she agreed to be in a relationship with me, because we had sought the face of God even before we began a relationship at all and I was too sure. So, I just wanted her to know that there was no going back for me. It was more of an act of faith than anything else. It was a cheap ring I could afford at the time, and thankfully I was getting married to a virtuous woman who wasn't overly concerned about material things. So, she wore it proudly, and I am sure a lot of people would have assumed it was just a fashion ring because it really didn't look like much, but it meant something to us. Fast forward, years later and I was able to take her to an expensive jewelry store just before our wedding to pick out the ring of her choice with which I re-engaged her. You must show commitment in some way.

There are young people who date for years without clearly defining their relationship. The entire thing is based on assumptions. The lady assumes that because they are always together and have 'all things common' like the disciples in Acts 2:44, they are in a romantic relationship. The guy assumes that the lady understands that the fact that they are always together does not mean they are in a committed relationship. And because the lady is either not courageous enough to ask the question bluntly, or is afraid of an answer that will break her heart, they go on in silence until so much time passes and eventually something has to give and then the bubble bursts. Please ask questions and make sure your relationship is defined. Are you just friends, best friends, close friends, in a relationship, in a serious relationship, in a courtship, or is your relationship status 'its complicated'? Anyone who is sincerely interested in having you for keeps will not be ashamed of you or hide your relationship. If there is secrecy, there is something wrong. Ask and demand. If he gets angry and leaves you, that is better than wasting all those years and eventually finding out that all he saw you as was "a sister". You may think because you kiss and make out with him, he should know you are in a relationship, but I assure you, there are no guarantees in this thing until a firm commitment is made, either verbally and in ways that can be seen. Some people who show commitment still end up breaking hearts, so how much more when you are simply floating? Be wise.

Covenant

Marriage is a covenant relationship
between three people.
You, Your Partner and God.

Marriage is a covenant relationship, and the highest form of covenant that exists between humans. It is a covenant between the two people involved, but it is also a covenant between them and God. God is the third person in a marriage relationship, and so you can say that marriage is a covenant relationship between three people. Therefore, it must not be taken lightly. God is interested in the success of your marriage because it brings glory and honour to His name. Don't forget this is His institution; the holy institution which He loves. It was His idea in the first place, and making it work says that God did not make a mistake. As with every covenant, each party is expected to fulfil their part of the agreement and there are blessings or rewards for doing so and consequences for breaking the covenant. It is the same with marriage. You must make up your mind to be faithful to the terms of this covenant if you want to get into it. You cannot go into marriage like the people who have it somewhere at the back of their minds that if it doesn't work they can just take a walk. That is not God's idea of a covenant. A covenant is something that binds people together and the terms are expected to be fulfilled regardless of the situation or circumstances. All the partners have a part to play. You cannot also go into marriage thinking it is okay to be unfaithful to your partner if the opportunity arises. Don't forget that it is not just about you and your partner anymore, but God is also involved in this covenant because it is His institution you are getting into. Even if your partner never finds out, God knows all you do and He rewards accordingly.

Copulation

The original intent of God for sex in marriage
is that two individuals who have
no previous sexual experiences
come together and learn and grow
together in the marriage bed.

Sex. I know you probably know more than I do about this subject. I am also tempted to assume that you already know, and agree, that this should only take place under the covenant covering of marriage, and you are committed to this truth. However, for the avoidance of doubt, let me state it again. Regardless of how the world views this, the standard of God hasn't changed. He frowns at fornication (2 Corinthians 6:18), no matter how many fancy names the world has given it, so it doesn't look so bad. Make up your mind that you will not engage in sex before marriage. It is a sin against God. It is also a sin against your body which is the dwelling place of God. And like we already established, there are consequences to everything we do while we are single, and most of these consequences wait for us in marriage. The biggest baggage that people take into marriage is their past sexual experiences.

In marriage however, sex is meant to be enjoyed, and to keep couples coming back to each other. Copulation is the consummation of a marriage. It is the highest form of human relationship and 'knowing' there is. That is why the bible says you become one flesh with any one you have sexual intercourse with (1 Corinthians 6:16). It is a very powerful thing that should not be taken lightly. Yet, it becomes a problem in marriage when it is not approached properly. If you go into marriage with multiple sexual experiences in your past, as the human being that you are, you will begin to make comparison that are unhealthy for your marriage. You begin to compare your partner to a previous sexual experience you have had, and you expect your partner to behave in a certain way forgetting that he or she is a completely different person made in the image and likeness of God.

The original intent of God for sex in marriage is that two individuals who have had no previous sexual experiences come together and learn and grow together in the marriage bed without the baggage and mind games of previous experiences. This is what he showed us with Adam and Eve and this should be our goal too. I know this is not the popular thing any more, but you can make up your mind that you will keep to the standard of God. Maybe you are reading this, and you are saying, "What if I have already done so much before I realised it was this serious?" You can choose to turn a new page now and ask God for a new beginning on this journey. You will need to renew your mind from this point forward, but one thing you don't want to do is to continue to join yourself to different people by sleeping around. We cannot continue in sin and expect the grace of God to abound towards us (Romans 6:1). Repentance is about turning from a sinful way and choosing to do the right thing.

You will also need to ask important questions about your partner's sexual preferences. As a child of God, you are not allowed to explore each other sexually, so you must make the most of your questions. Ask the right questions and pay attention. Refuse to be deceptive or give the wrong impression about your sexual preference just to please your partner. You must be truthful about such conversations because sex is a leading cause of broken marriages.

These days, it has also become important to ask (and if need be, to investigate) your partner's sexual orientation. You can no longer assume that he or she is truly straight – interested in the opposite sex only – you must be sure.

The story of a reputable clergy who recently came out as gay might interest you. What was surprising about the whole episode was not that he claimed to be gay after so many years of preaching and teaching along with his wife, but the fact that he claimed to have told his wife that he was gay before they got married and they still got married and carried on for years. The truth is that people get married for different reasons, ranging from the selfish to the out rightly ridiculous, so you must watch and pray. Not a lot of people understand what marriage is and how important a decision it is. Some just get married because that is what is expected of you after a certain age. Some people get married because that is the supposed legitimate way to have regular sex and/or raise children. Others get married to take attention away from themselves and cover up their sexual orientation while others may get married hoping that this will help them overcome their desire for the same sex. There are also those who marry just to please their parents and family members. So many reasons. You have to be careful and prayerful, that is the best way to go about this journey of finding and choosing the right partner because marriage is a life long journey.

I wish you the very best.

This Thing Called Love

I had never seen Edwin cry.

I never really realised it until now, sitting in front of me, sobbing gently, my tough friend of fifteen years was being humbled by the one thing that most men would rather hide – emotions.

"Tell me what happened?" I asked again, as if he had not already told me that nothing new happened recently, except that things had really gone sour between his wife of three years, and himself.

"She has changed. I don't think I love her anymore," he said after a deep breath, "She wrote the same thing in that chat," he added, referring to a chat he had seen on his wife's phone where she was also expressing resignation over the situation with her husband to her childhood friend.

Love.

That word. It is probably the most misused word amongst young people.

"Did you ever love her?" I probed. I knew their story, so I was sure he knew where I was coming from. Himself and Sandra had met through a mutual friend of theirs and hit things off almost immediately. Butterflies. Sparks. All the works. Within months, Edwin was asking me for proposal ideas.

"Take it easy, man," I remember cautioning him severally.

"I love Sandra. You don't understand."

"Do you?"

"Yes. She is the best girl I have ever dated. Besides, we've been together for six months now..."

"Six years?" I cut in mockingly, "Oh, six months, wow! What a long time. Have you seen the worst of her yet?"

"You don't know how we feel about each other."

Feelings. I have no problem with your feelings. They are valid. But they are just that – feelings. Feelings do not mean Love. Attraction is very valid, but it is what it is – attraction. It does not mean you love someone. And no, she did not change. He just didn't court her long enough or well enough to see this side of her. It was all probably based on how they felt about each other at the time, forgetting that those feelings were based on certain actions. Haven't you ever had 'feelings' for someone and after some time, when the person wasn't responding in a way that could help the feelings grow, you gave up and moved on to someone else? The feelings probably did what they do best. Fade.

"We've had this discussion before Edwin. Marriage is not about feelings."

"You're always saying that. At least you are married. Didn't you have feelings for your wife?"

"Of course, I did, and I still do, but my point to you is that feelings and love are two different things. They take a stroll together occasionally and fool us into thinking they are a couple, but they are not. Forget the way we use the word love these days, love is much more than that."

"Preach...Pastor..."

"Call me what you like, but I bet you, if you listen to what I am telling you, in a few years, you will be glad you did.

"So you don't say I am preaching to you. Read First Corinthians 13 in the Message Bible, and see what love really is, then compare it to what you 'feel' for Sandra and come back and tell me if you really love her."

I bet he never read it.

God is love. What that means is that, if you want to know what love really is, you should look at the attributes of God. I opened the Bible app on my phone and began to read the passage out to him.

"Listen to this," I started to read from the description of love around the fourth verse.

Love never gives up.
Love cares more for others than for self.
Love doesn't want what it doesn't have.
Love doesn't strut,
Doesn't have a swelled head,
Doesn't force itself on others,
Isn't always "me first,"
Doesn't fly off the handle,
Doesn't keep score of the sins of others,
Doesn't revel when others grovel,
Takes pleasure in the flowering of truth,
Puts up with anything,
Trusts God always,
Always looks for the best,
Never looks back,
But keeps going to the end.
Love never dies.

"Can you die for Sandra?" I asked from the blues. I guess I was inspired by the last word I had read out. "Can you die in her place if it ever came to that, knowing that she may even turn around and marry your friend after your funeral?"

He didn't respond.

"Can you? Or can you even give one of your organs to her without hesitation to start with? Do you put her interests before yours? Are you committed to her, regardless of whatever you discover about her and whatever happens to her in the future? Love puts up with anything. It keeps going to the end. It never dies. So, you see that most of what we call love is really just attraction, and at best, infatuation?"

Love is a decision. It is something that grows with knowledge. It is not the same as Chemistry. It is much more than that.

Love is God.

God is love.
What that means is that, if you want
to know what love really is,
you should look at the attributes of God.